Merry

CHRISTMAS

This Books Belongs To

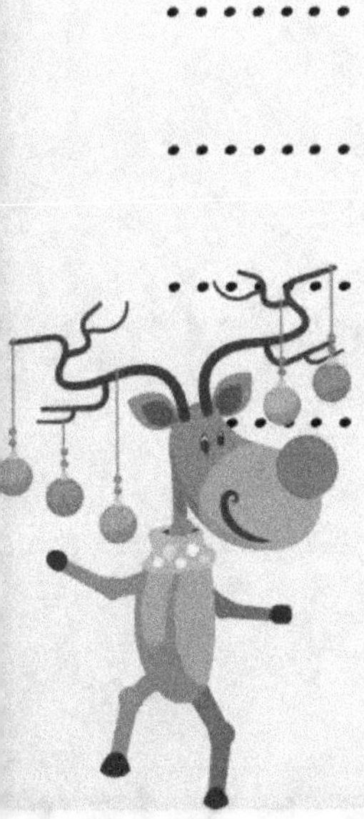

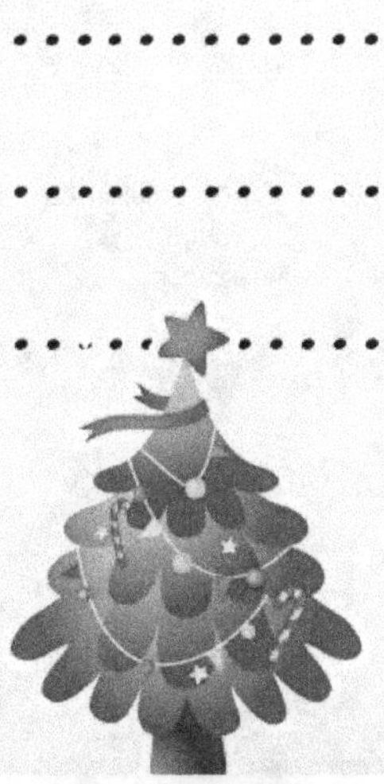

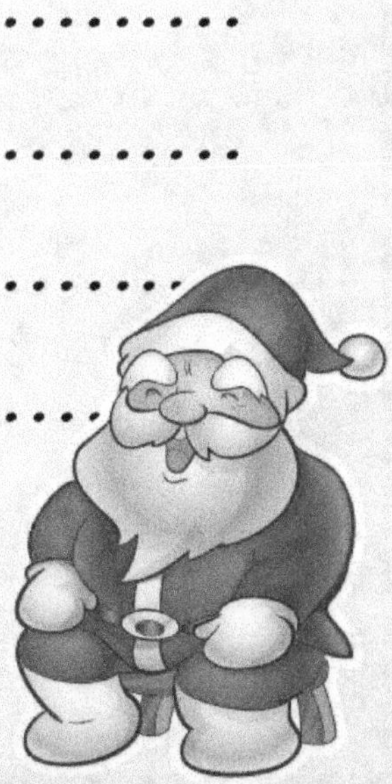

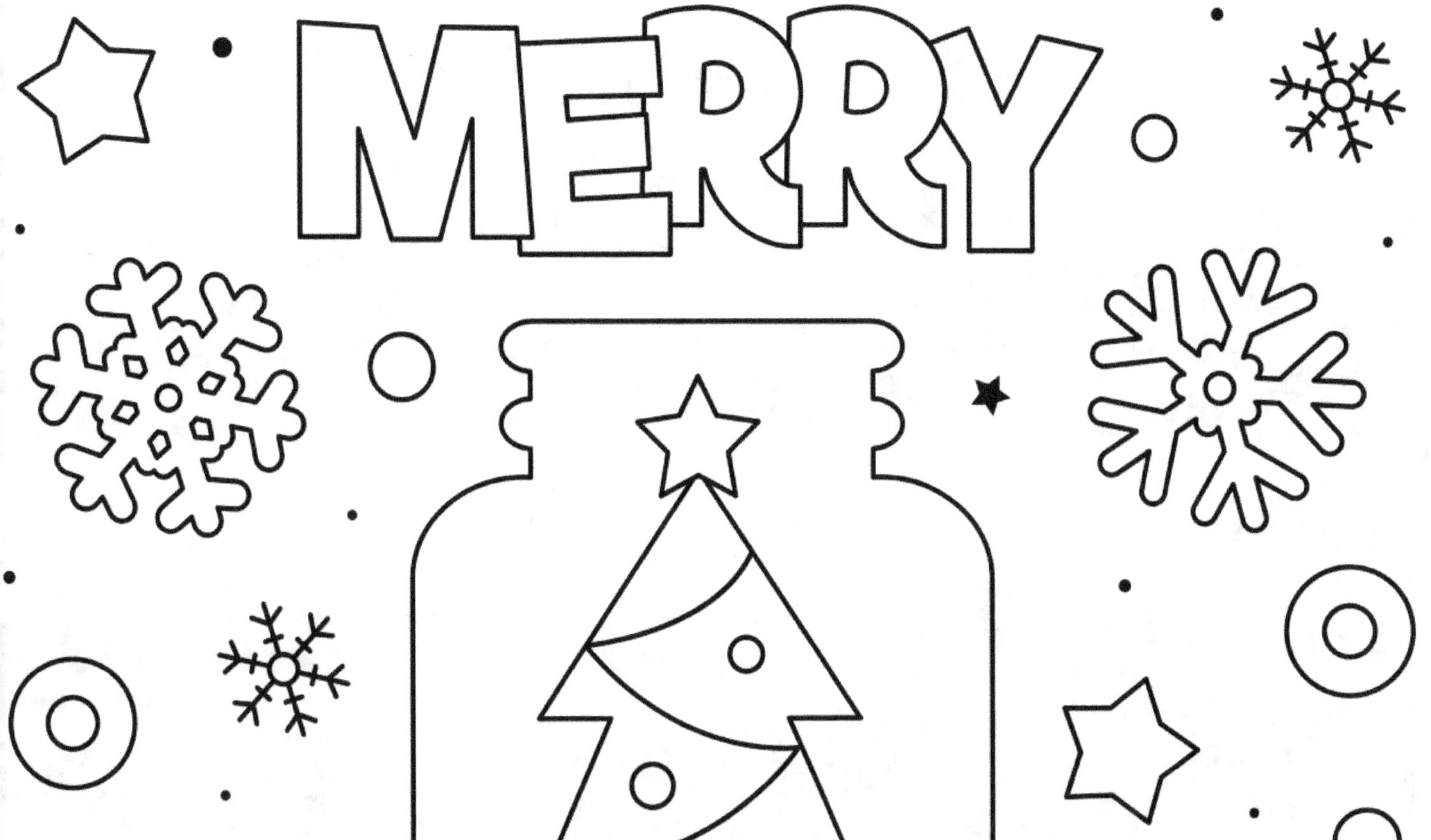
MERRY
CHRISTMAS

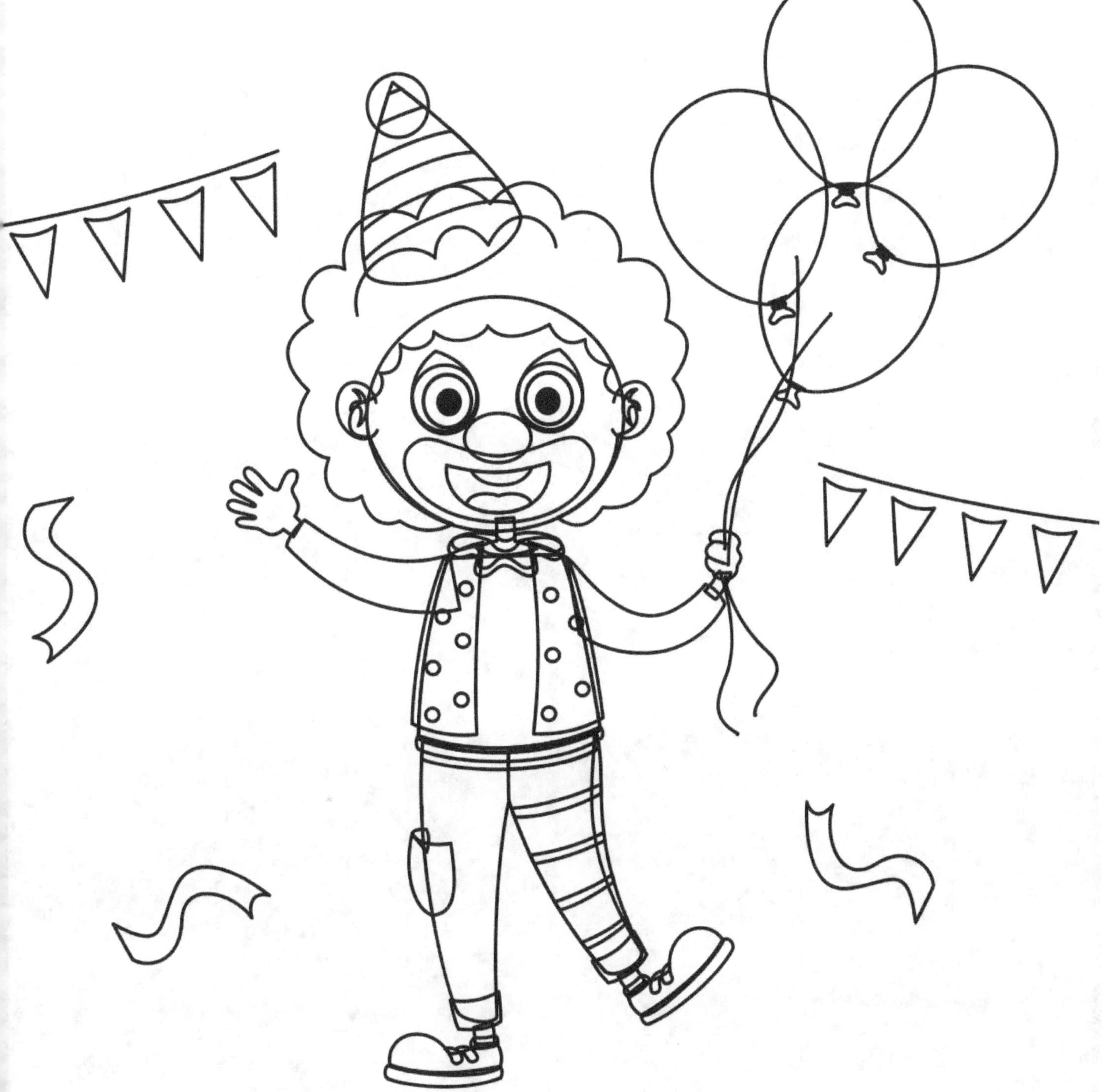

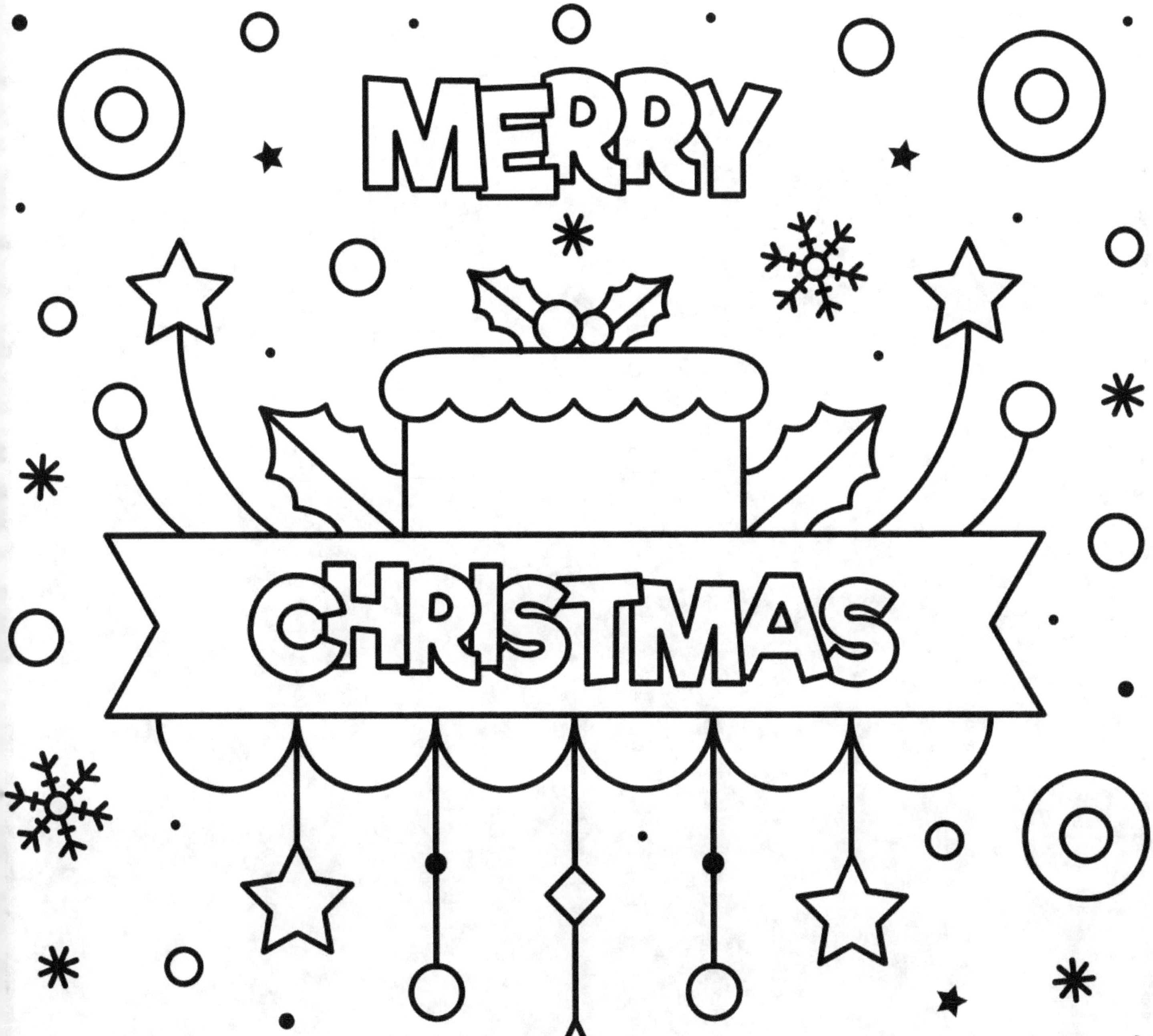
MERRY
CHRISTMAS

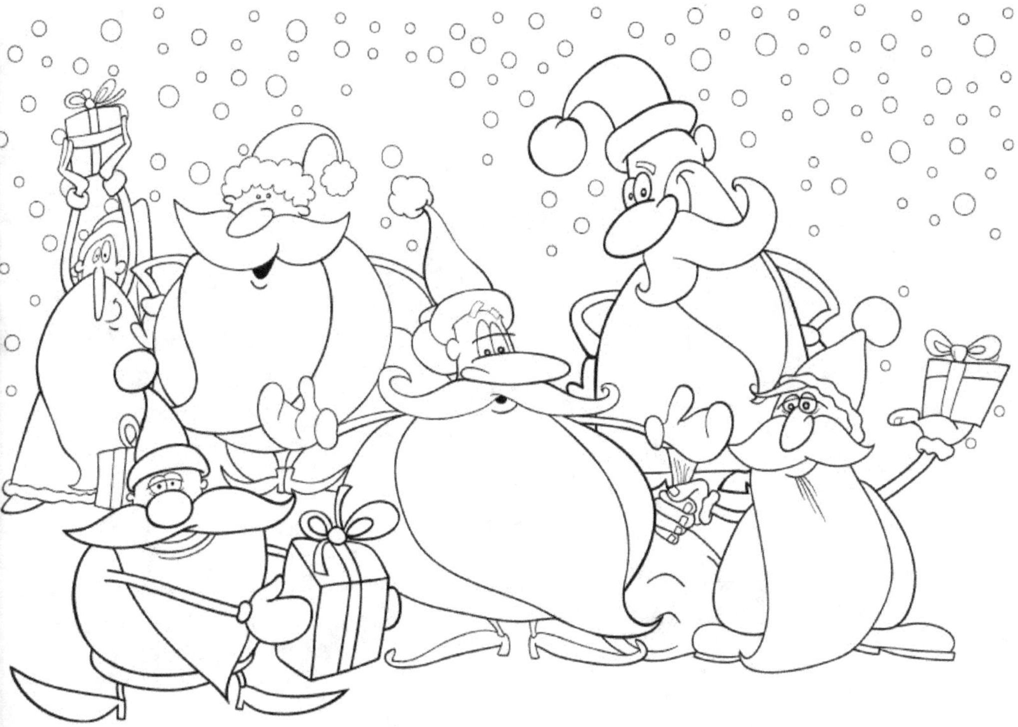

FIND 7 DIFFERENCES

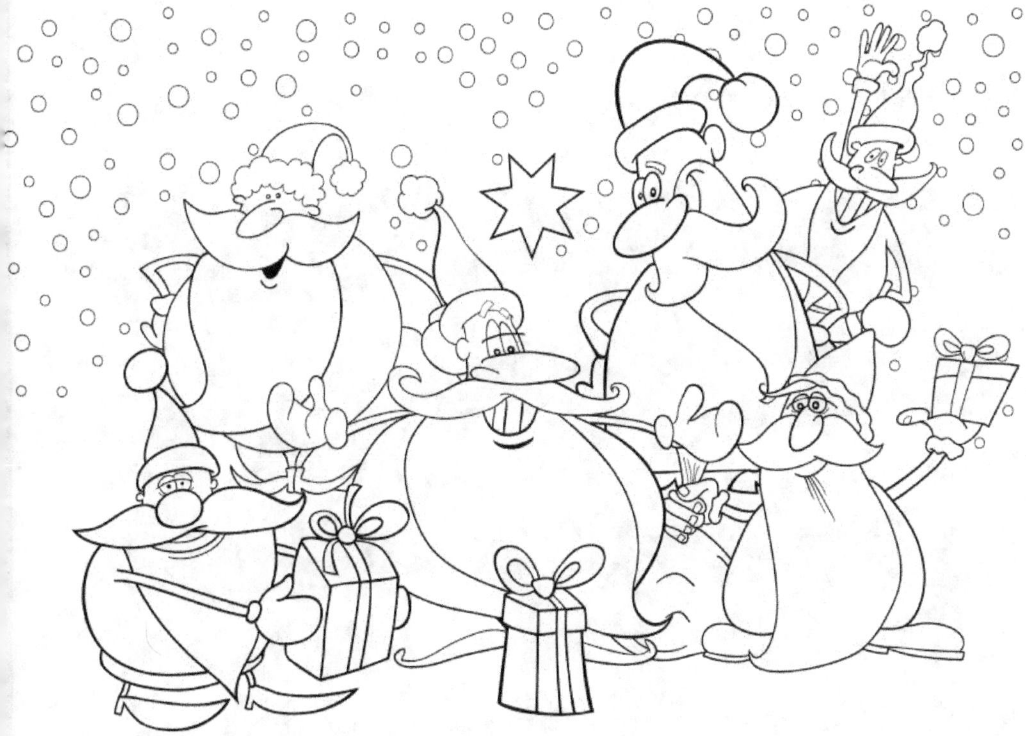

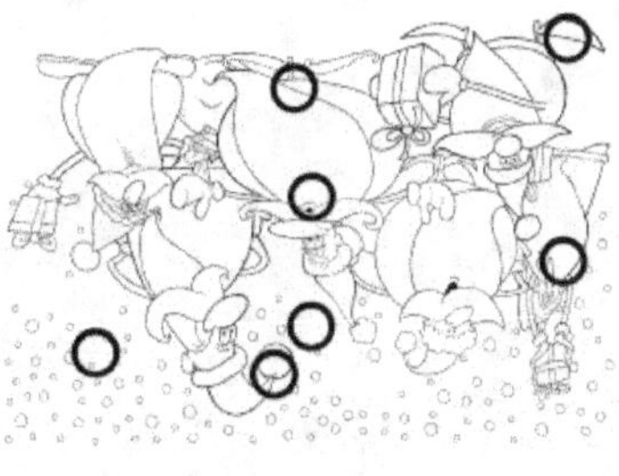

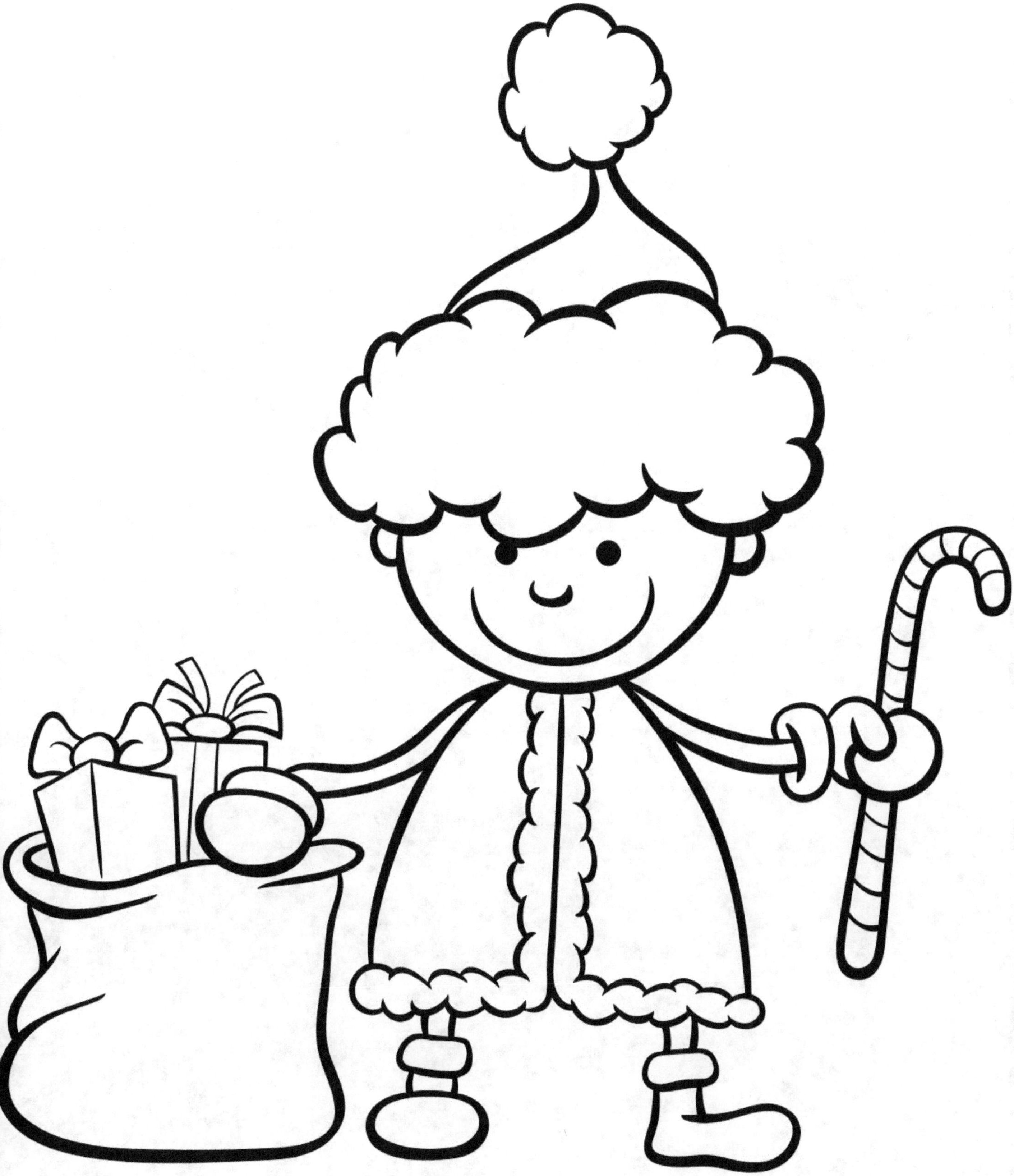

COLORING BOOK

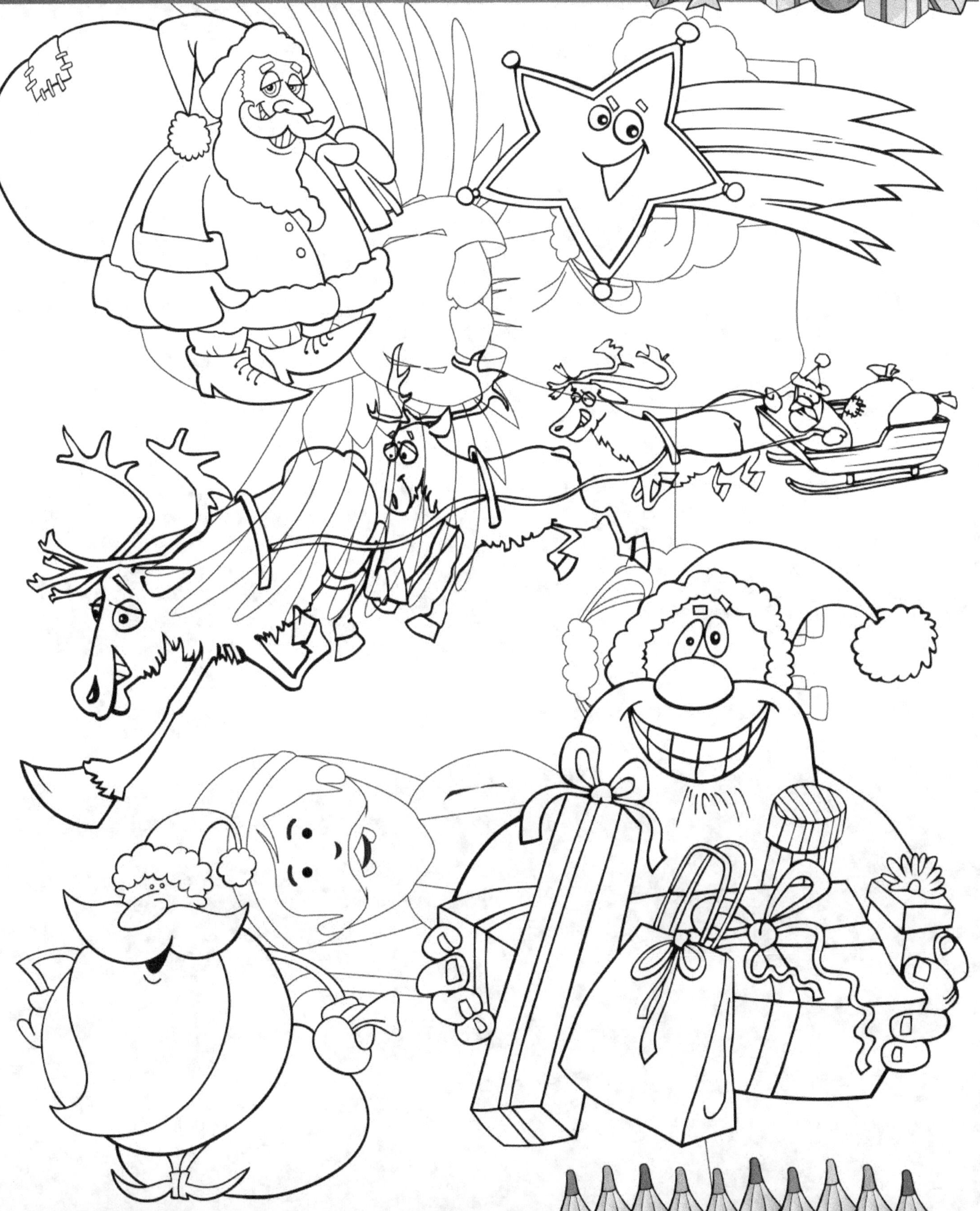

★ MERRY CHRISTMAS

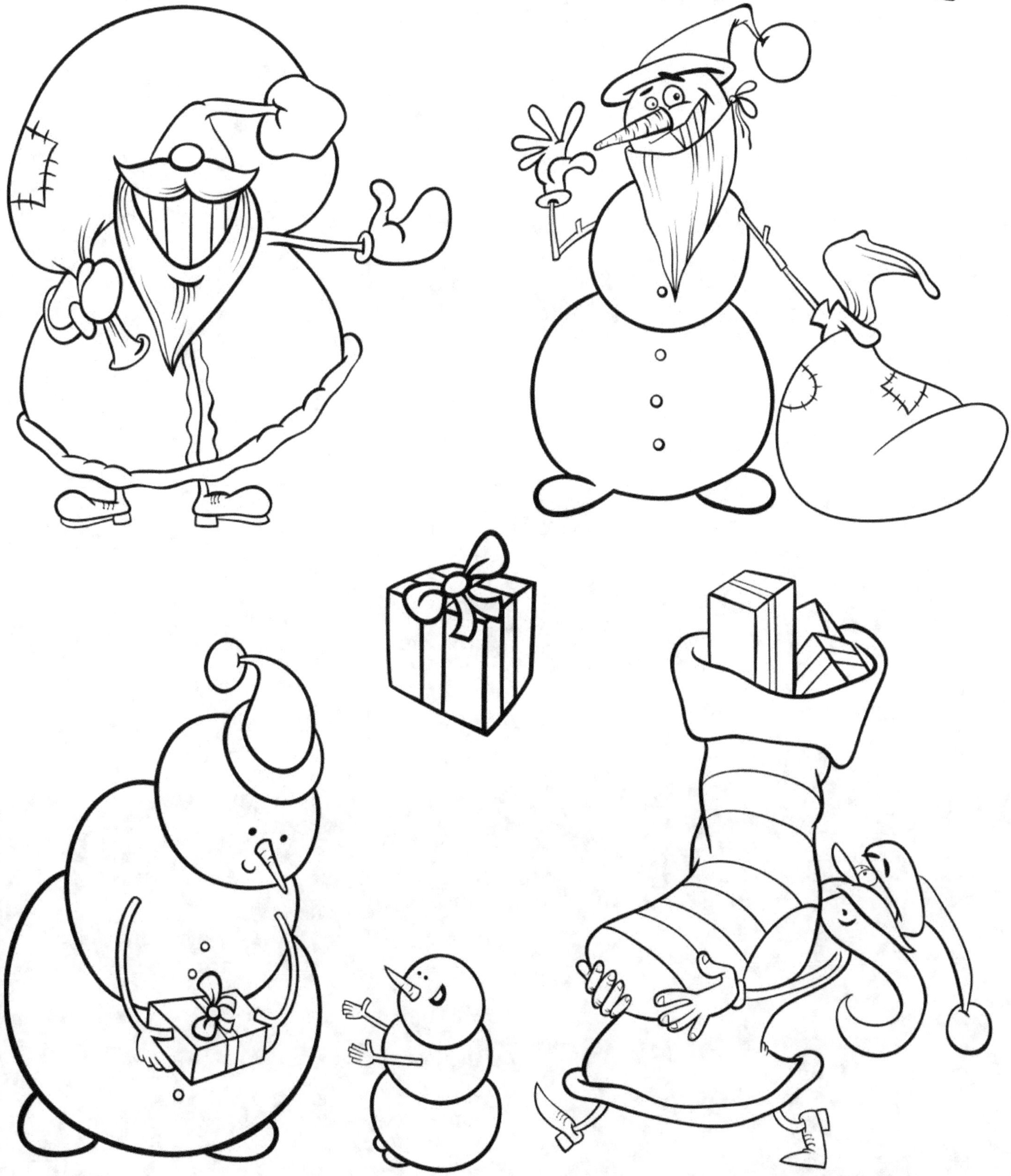

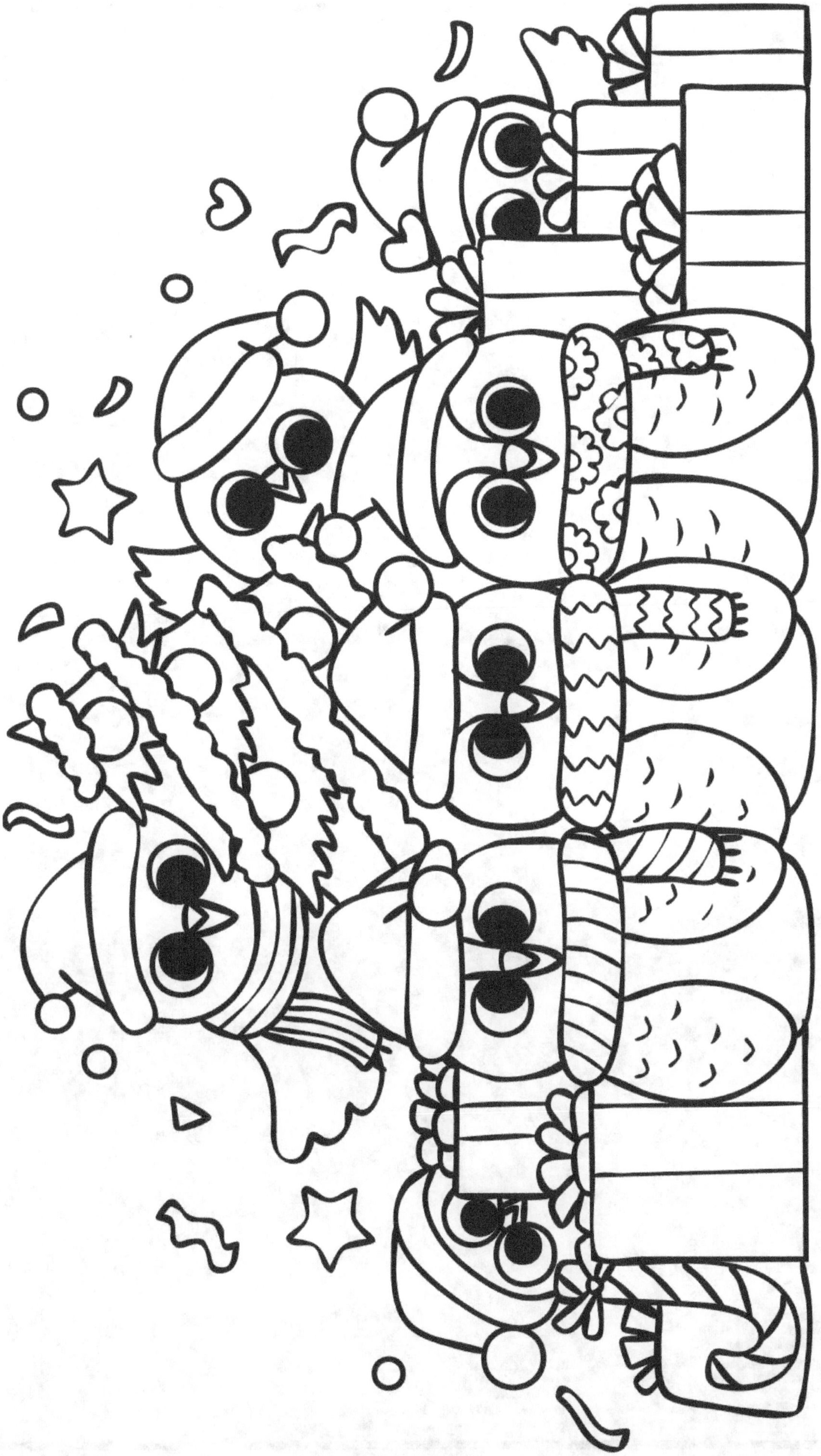

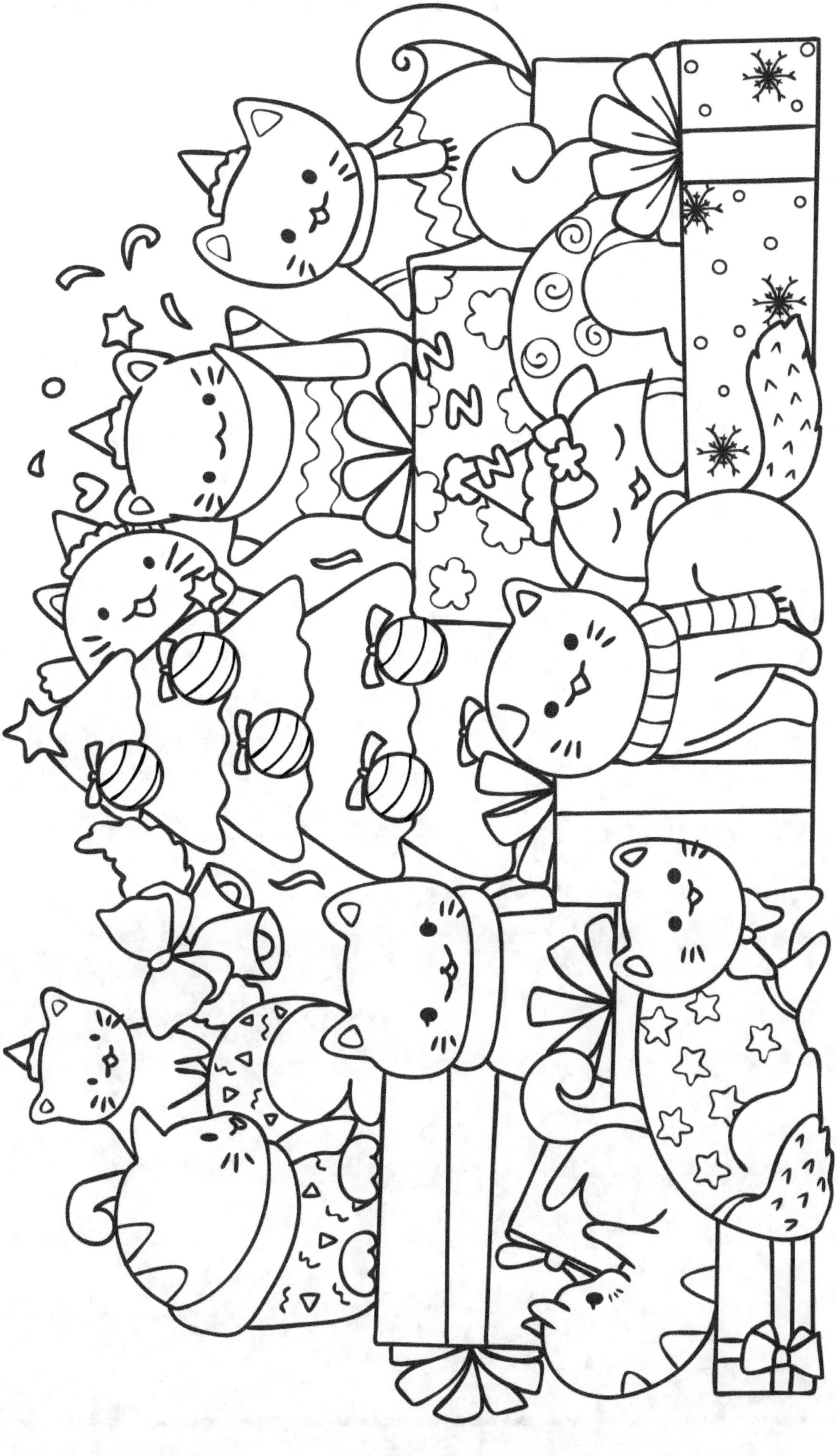
Z Z Z

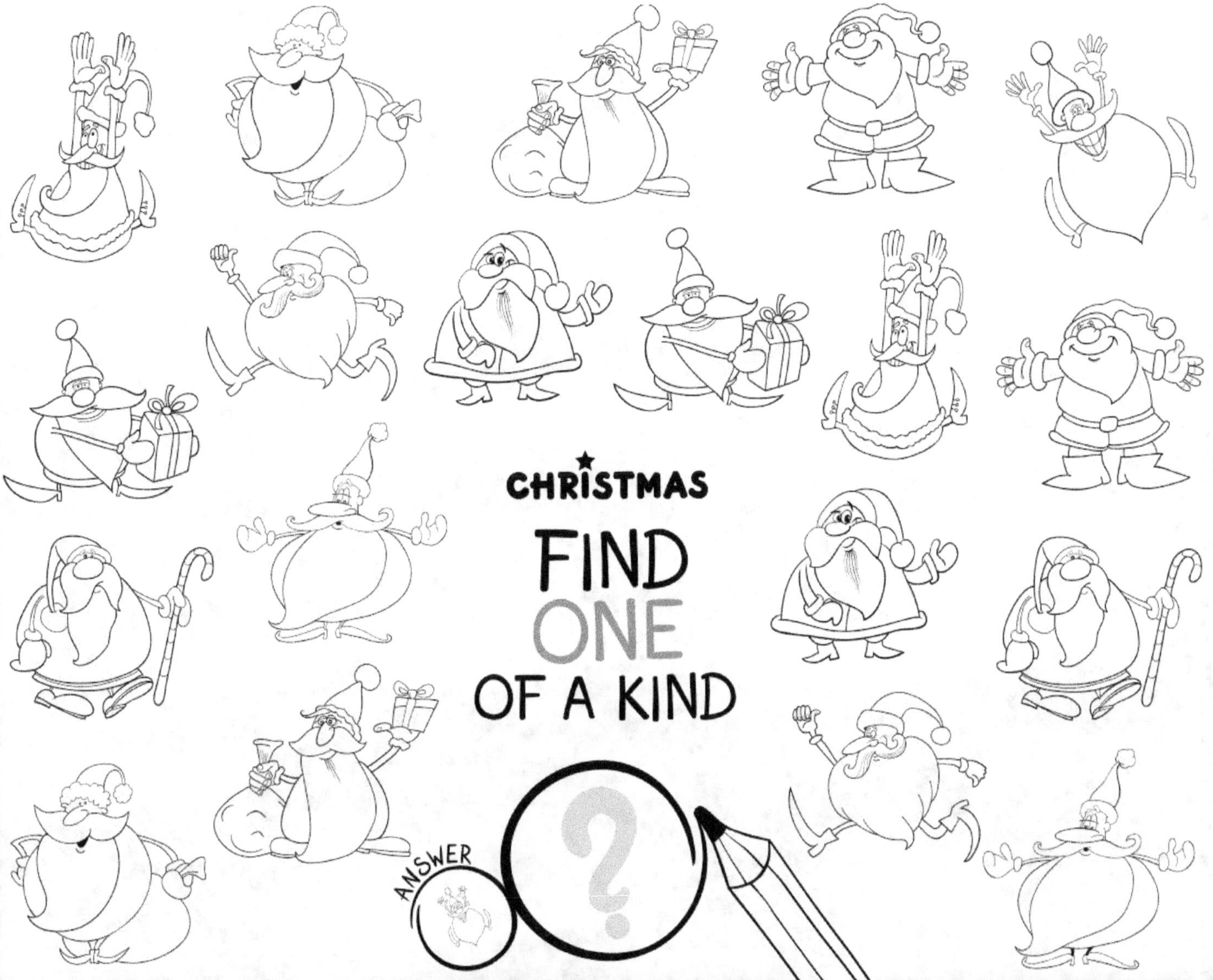
CHRISTMAS
FIND
ONE
OF A KIND
ANSWER

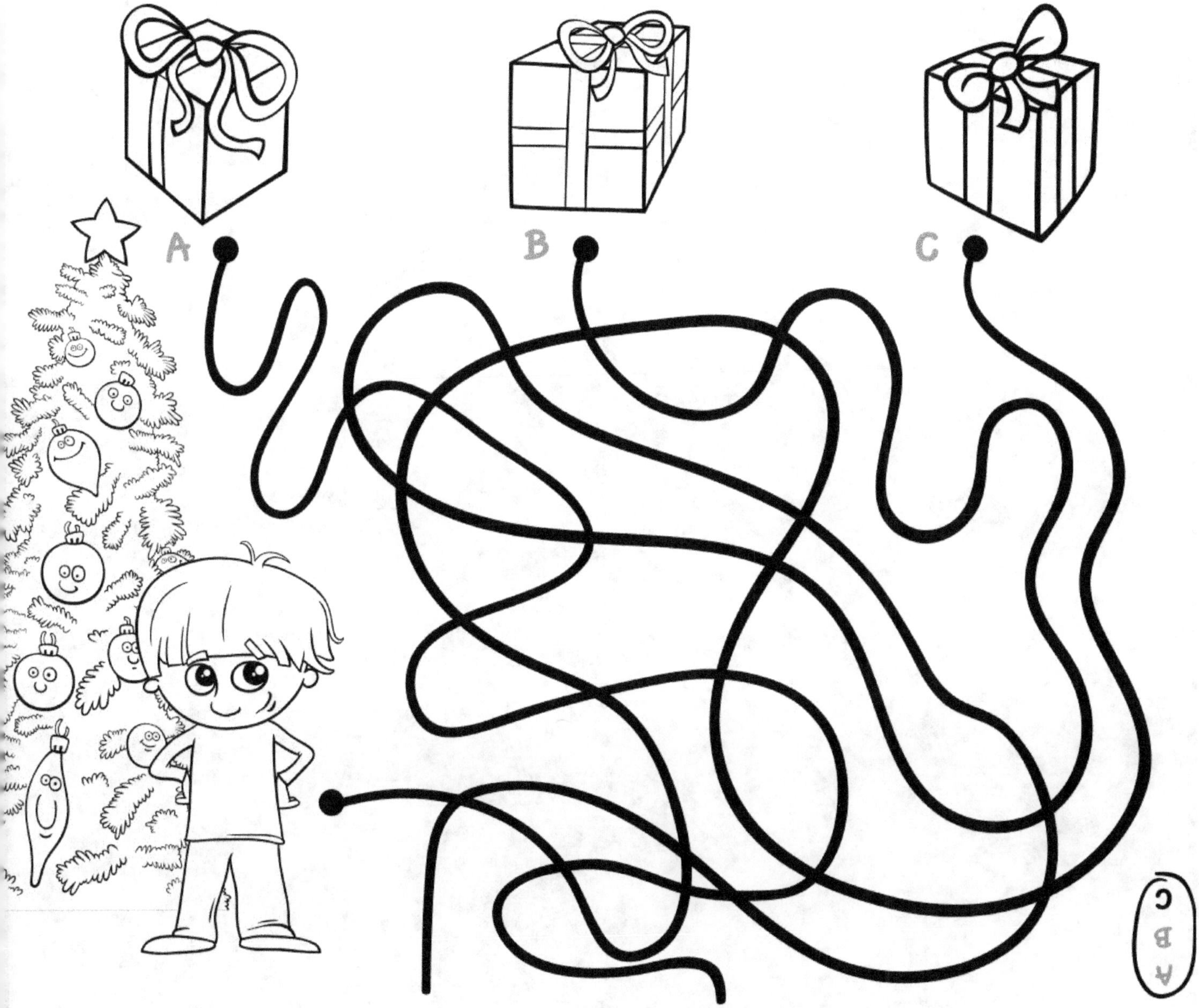
A
B
C

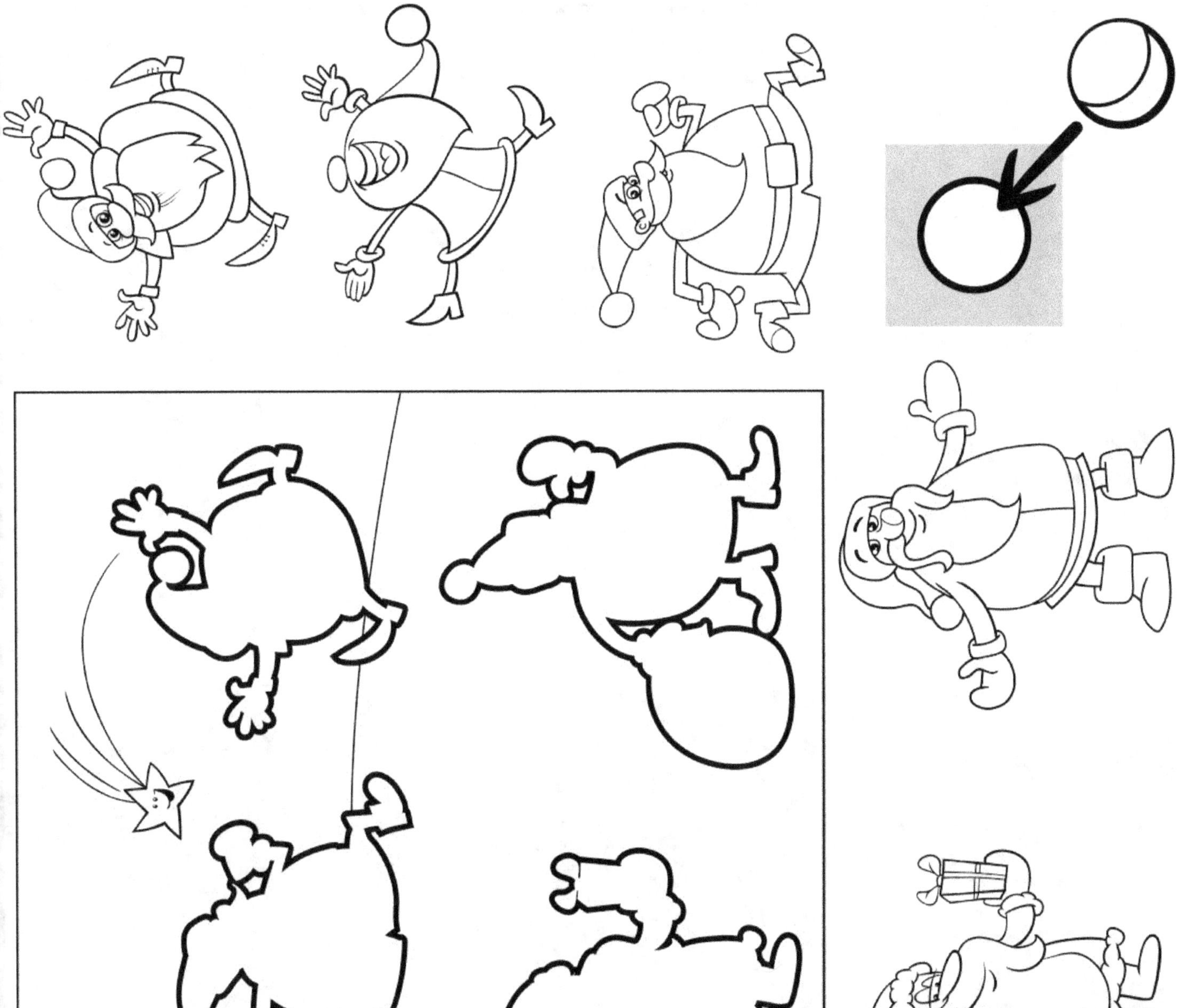

1

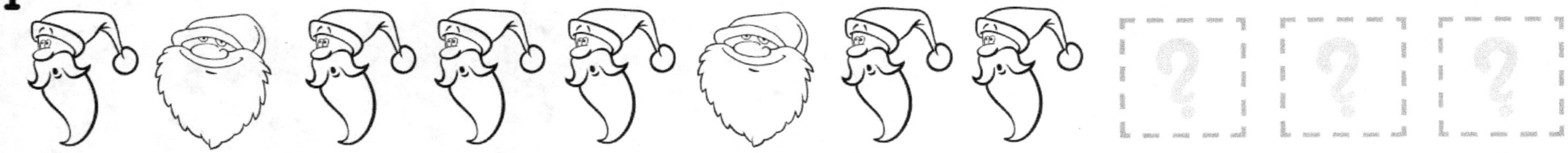

2

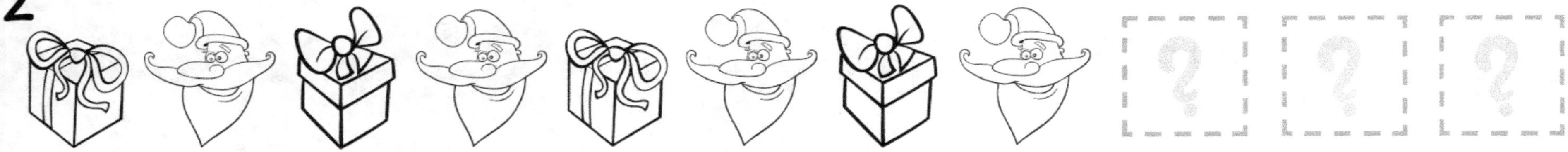

3

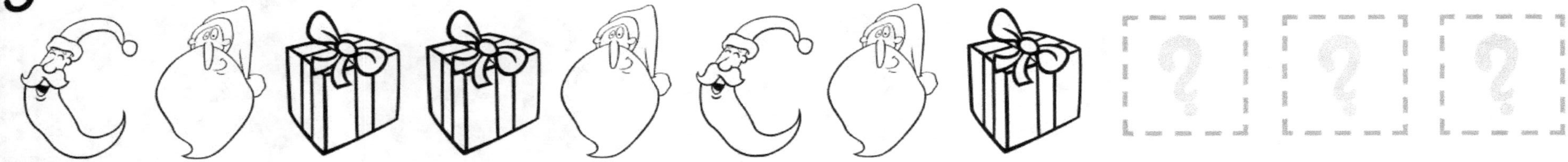

4

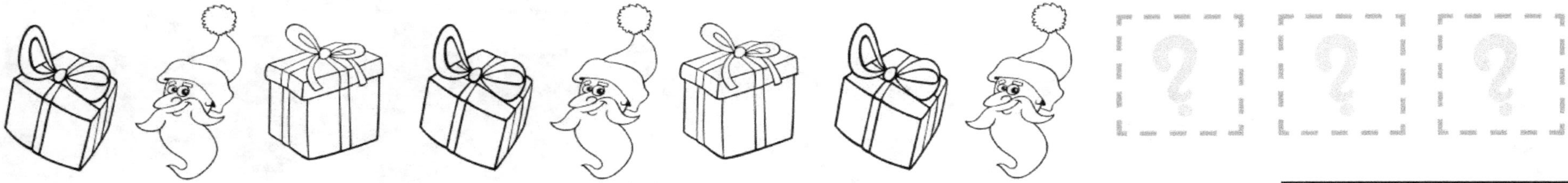

WHAT COMES NEXT?

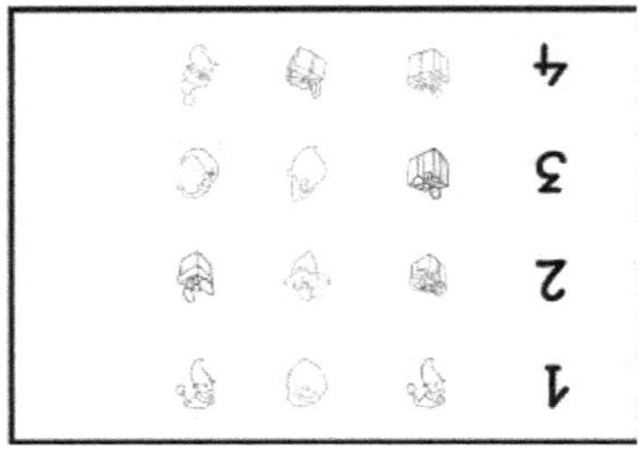

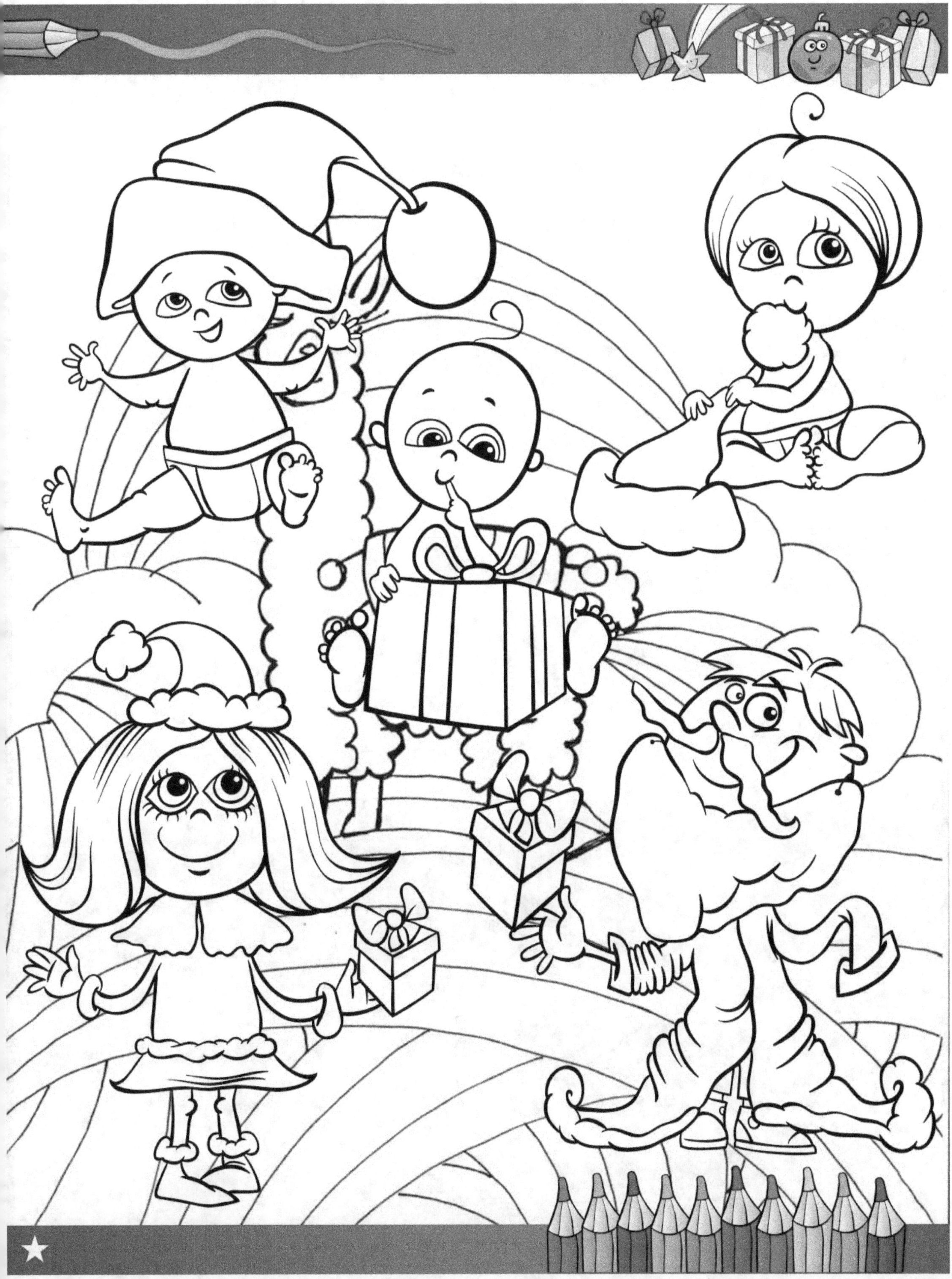

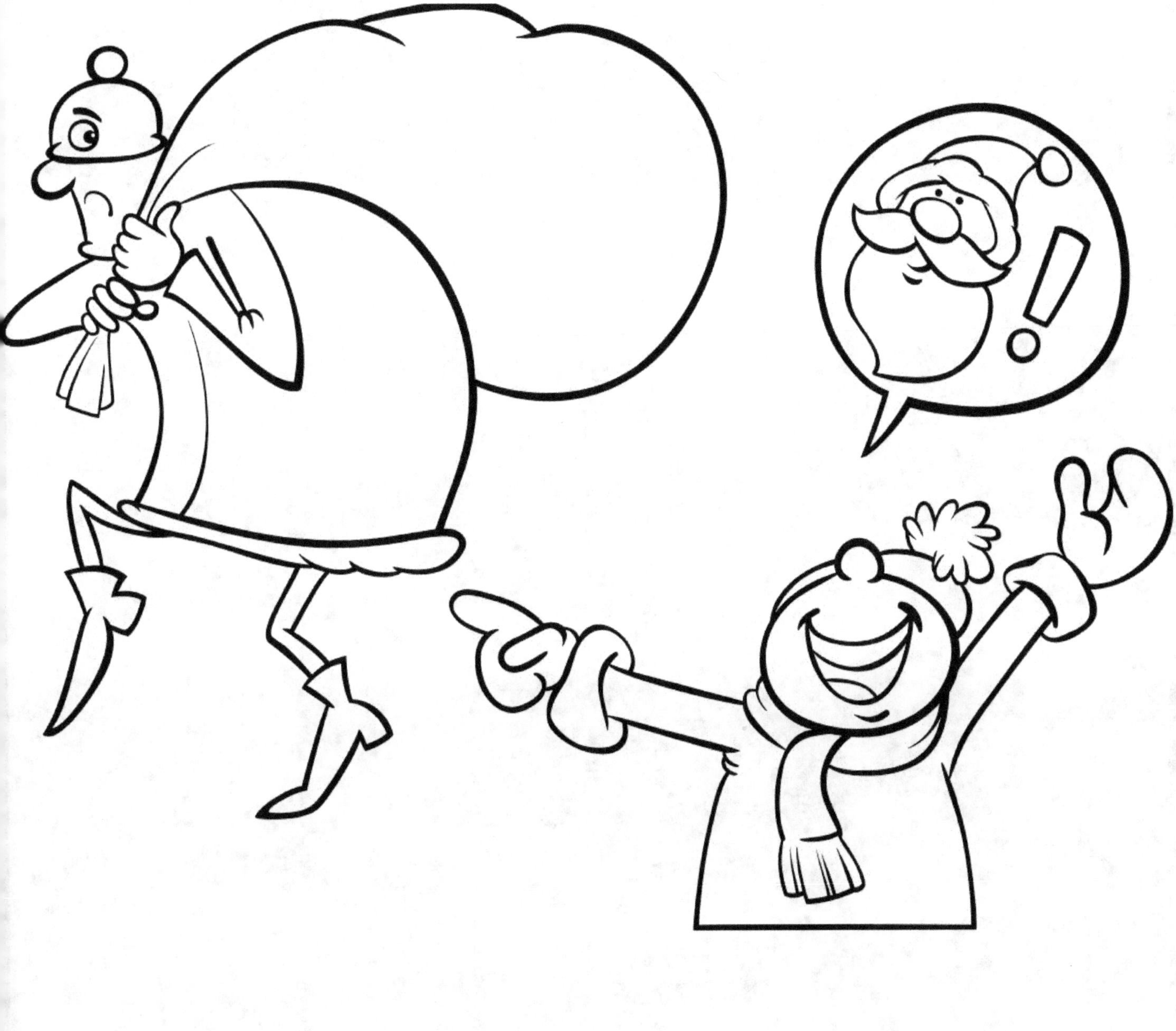

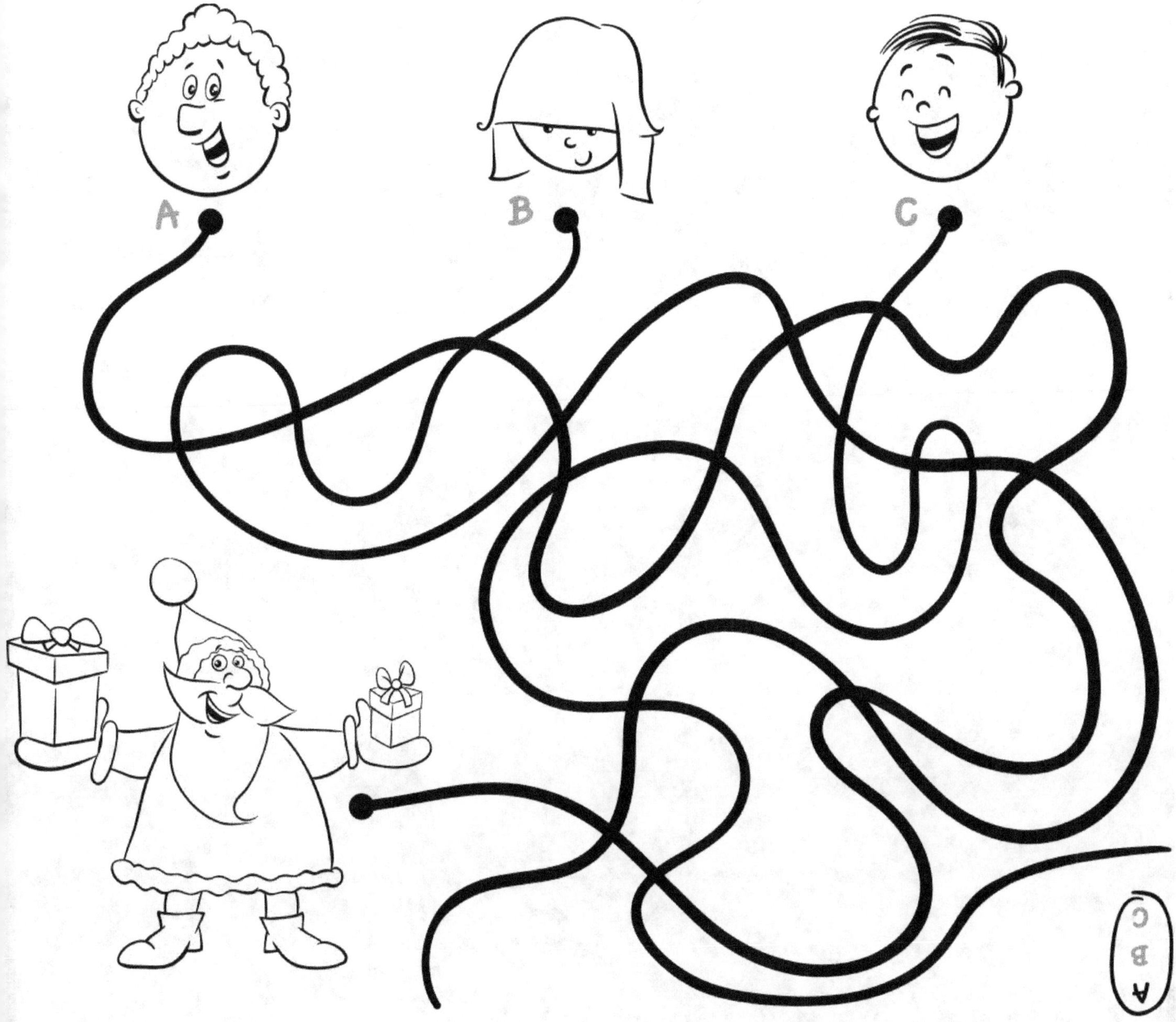

A
B
C

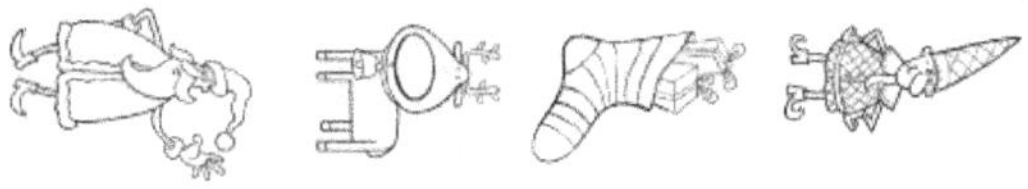

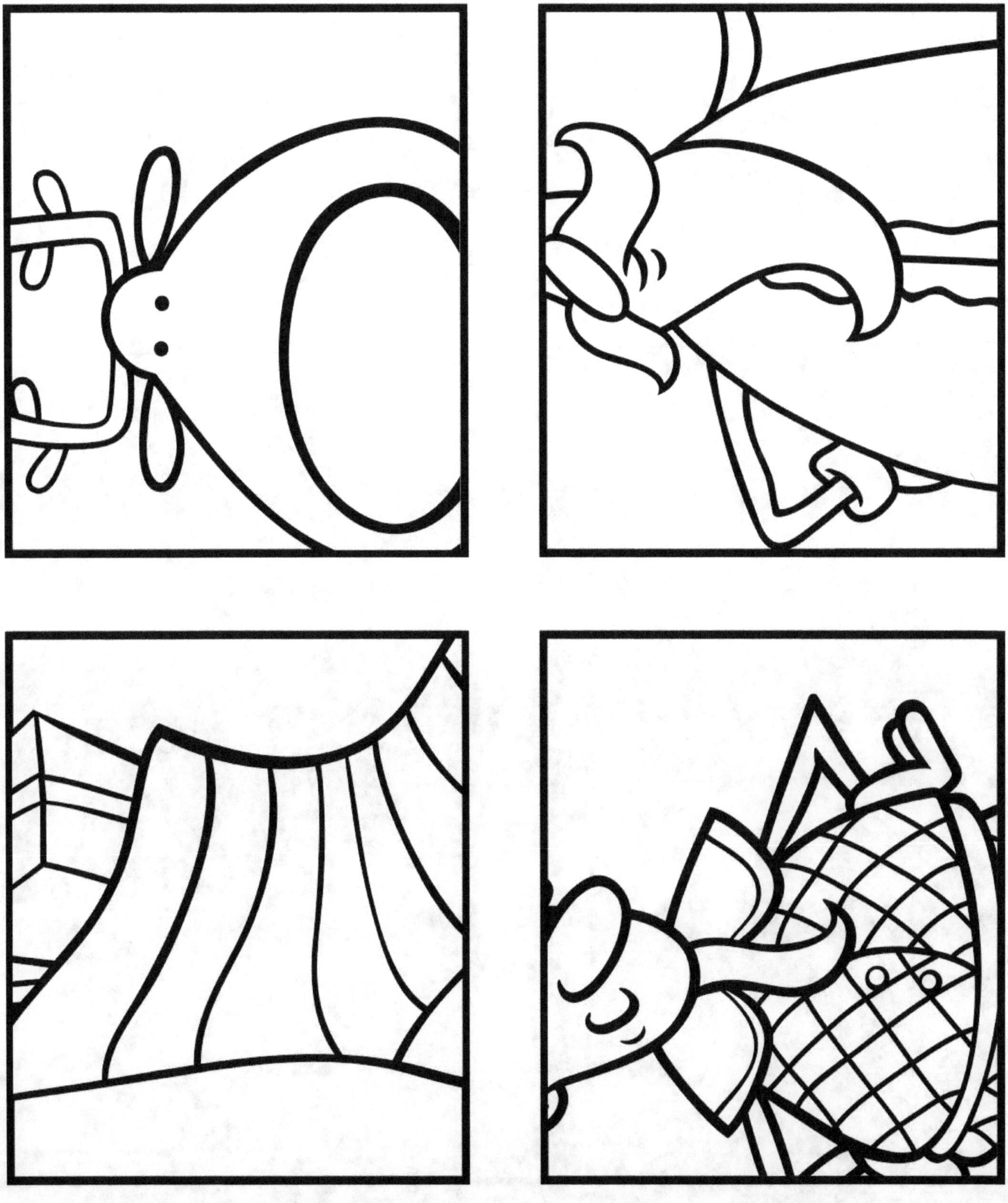

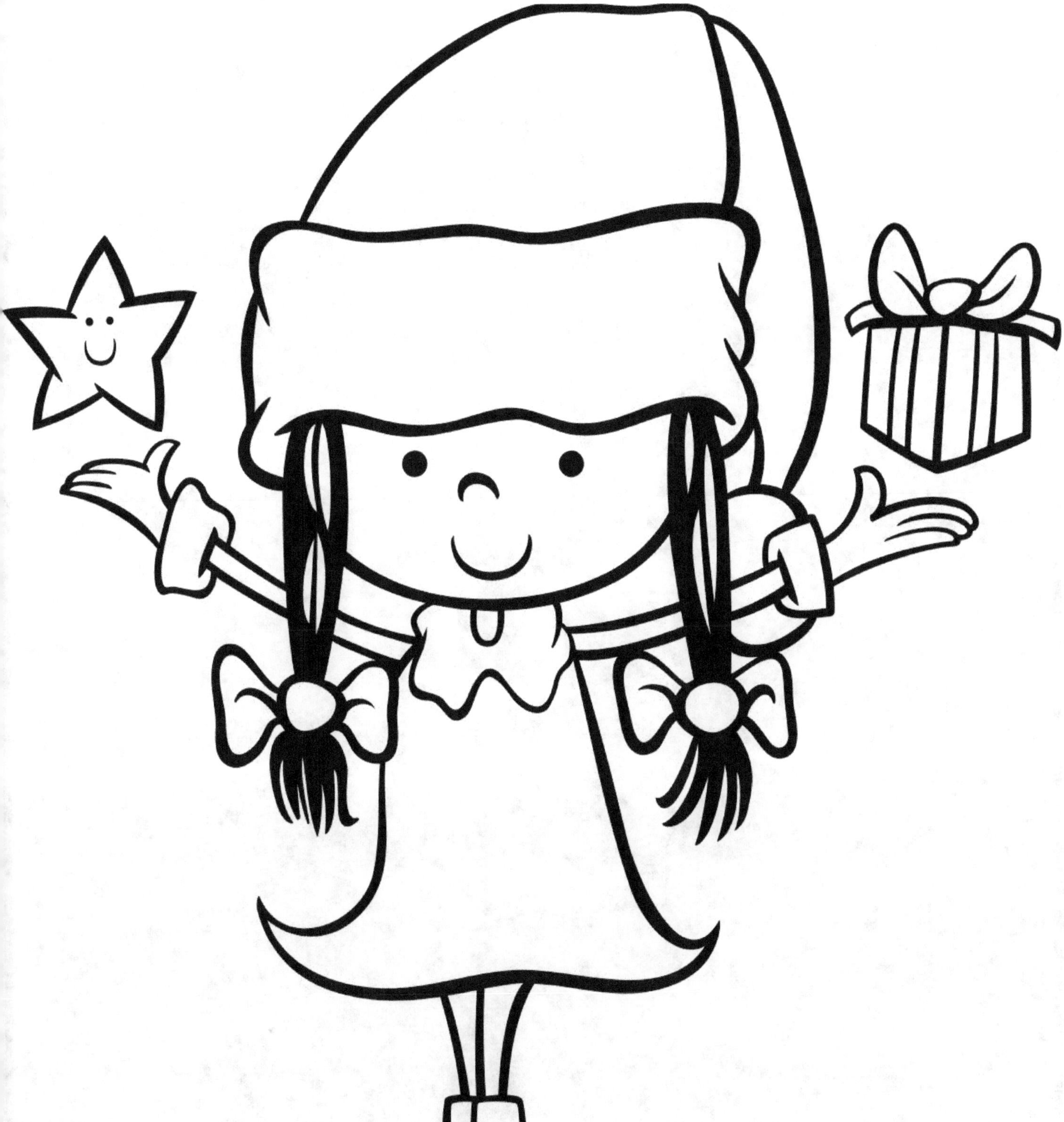

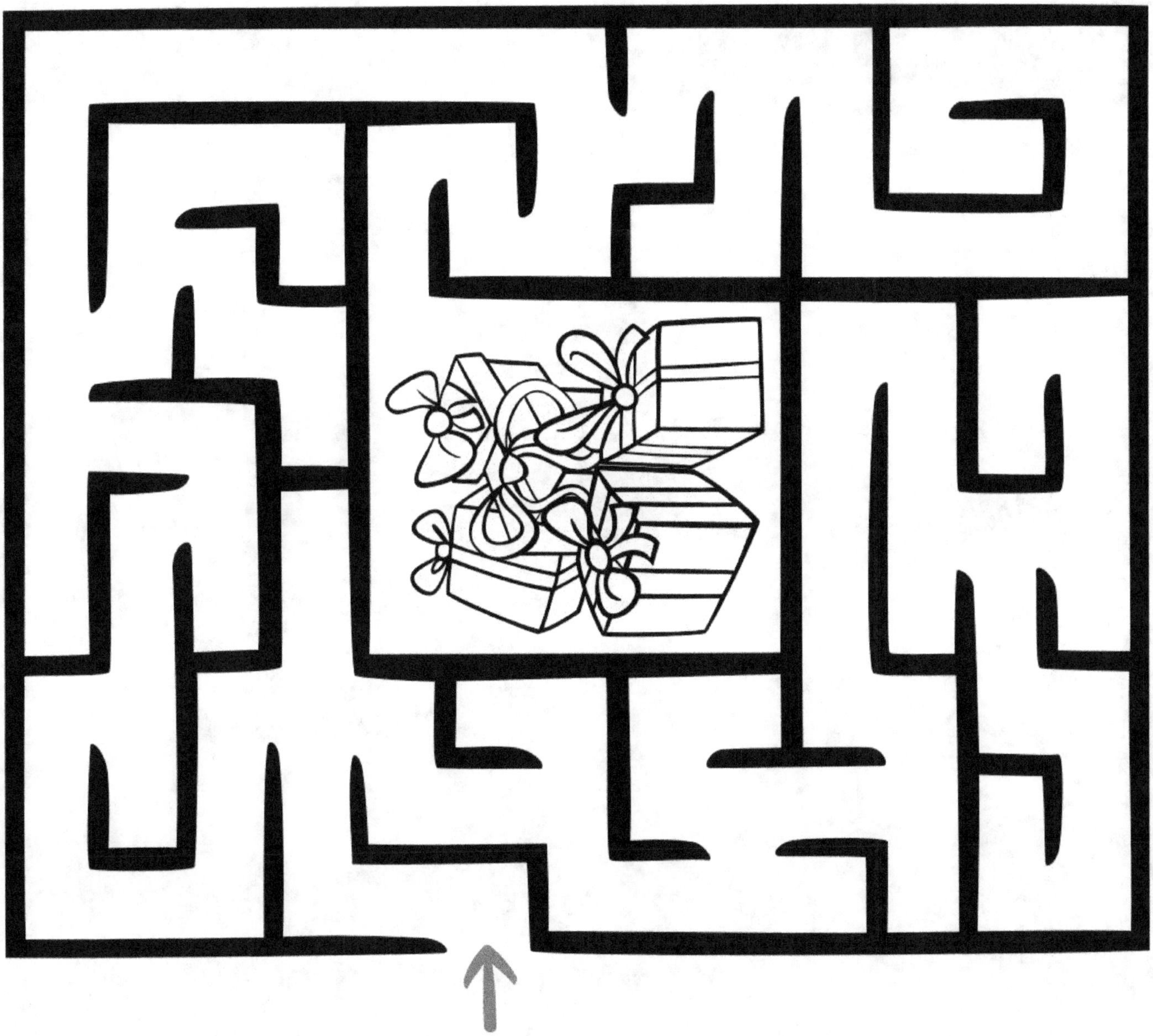

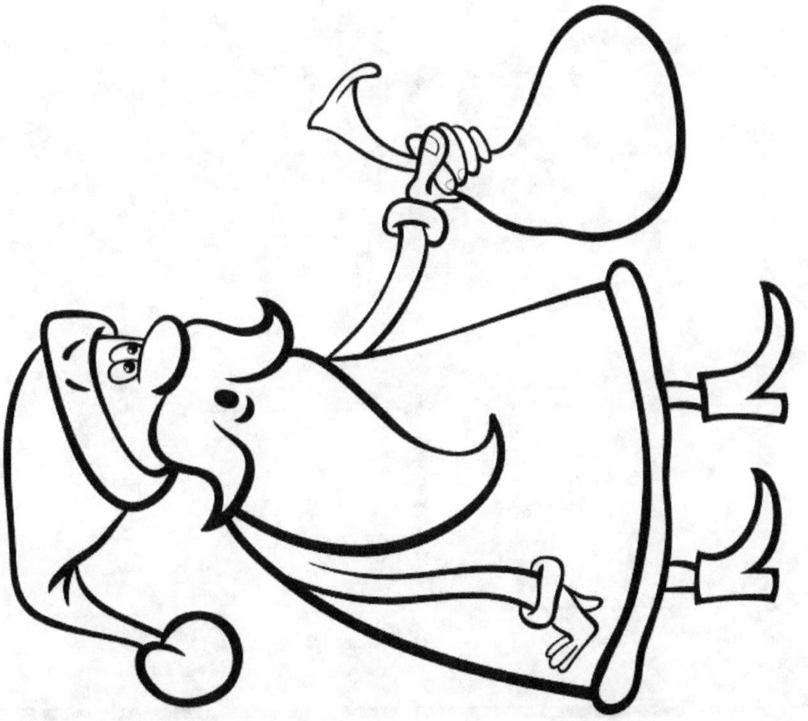

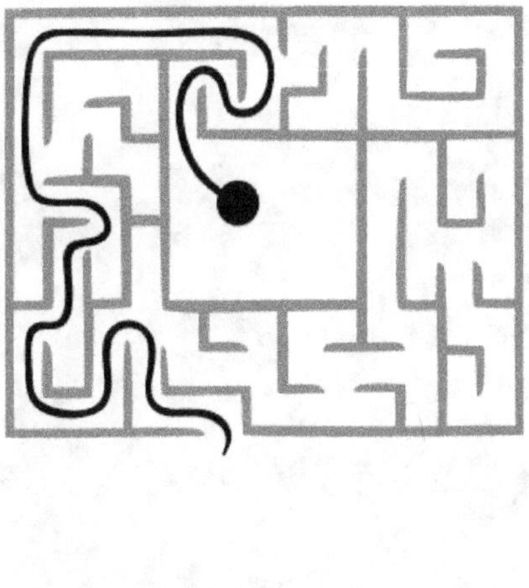

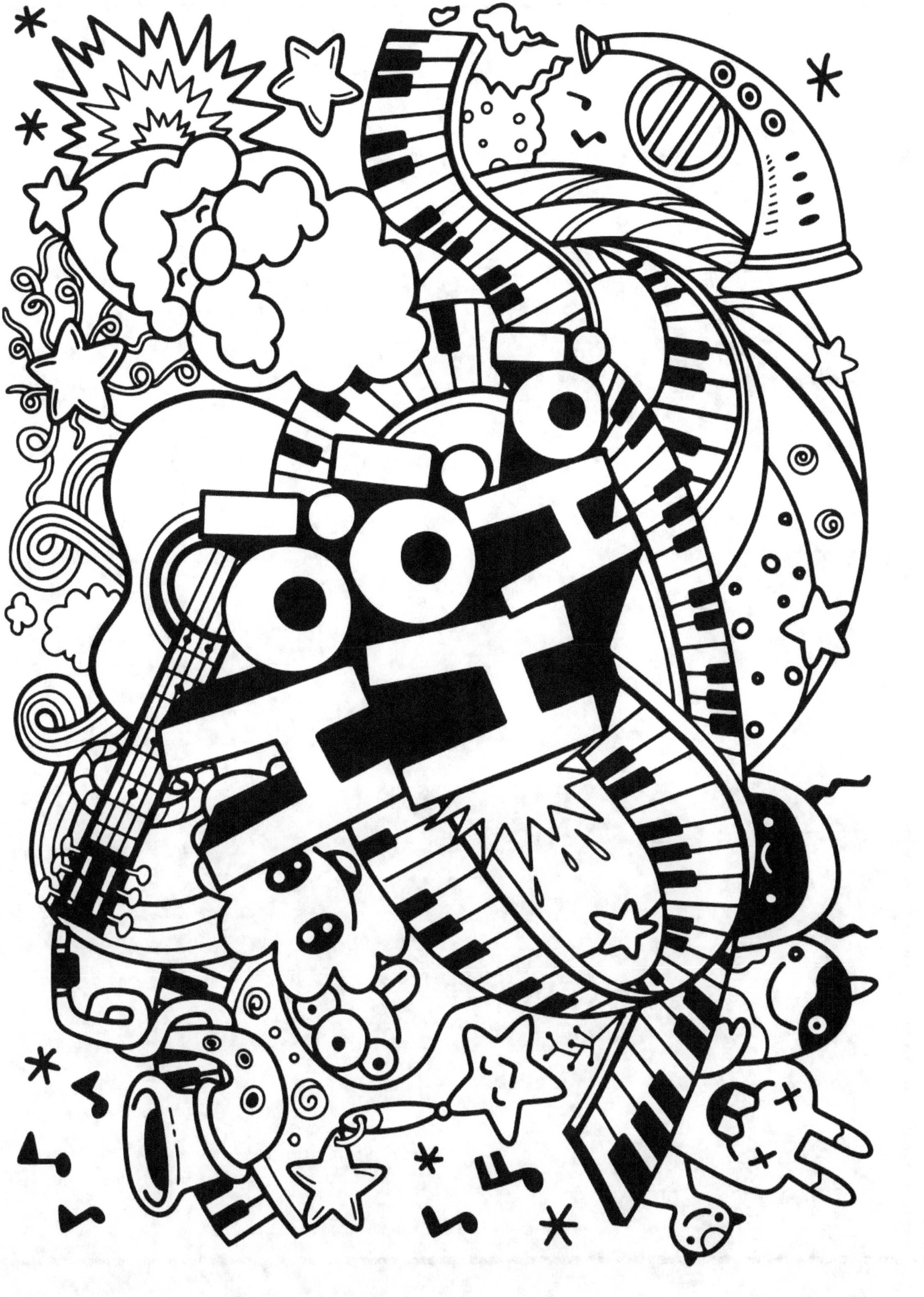

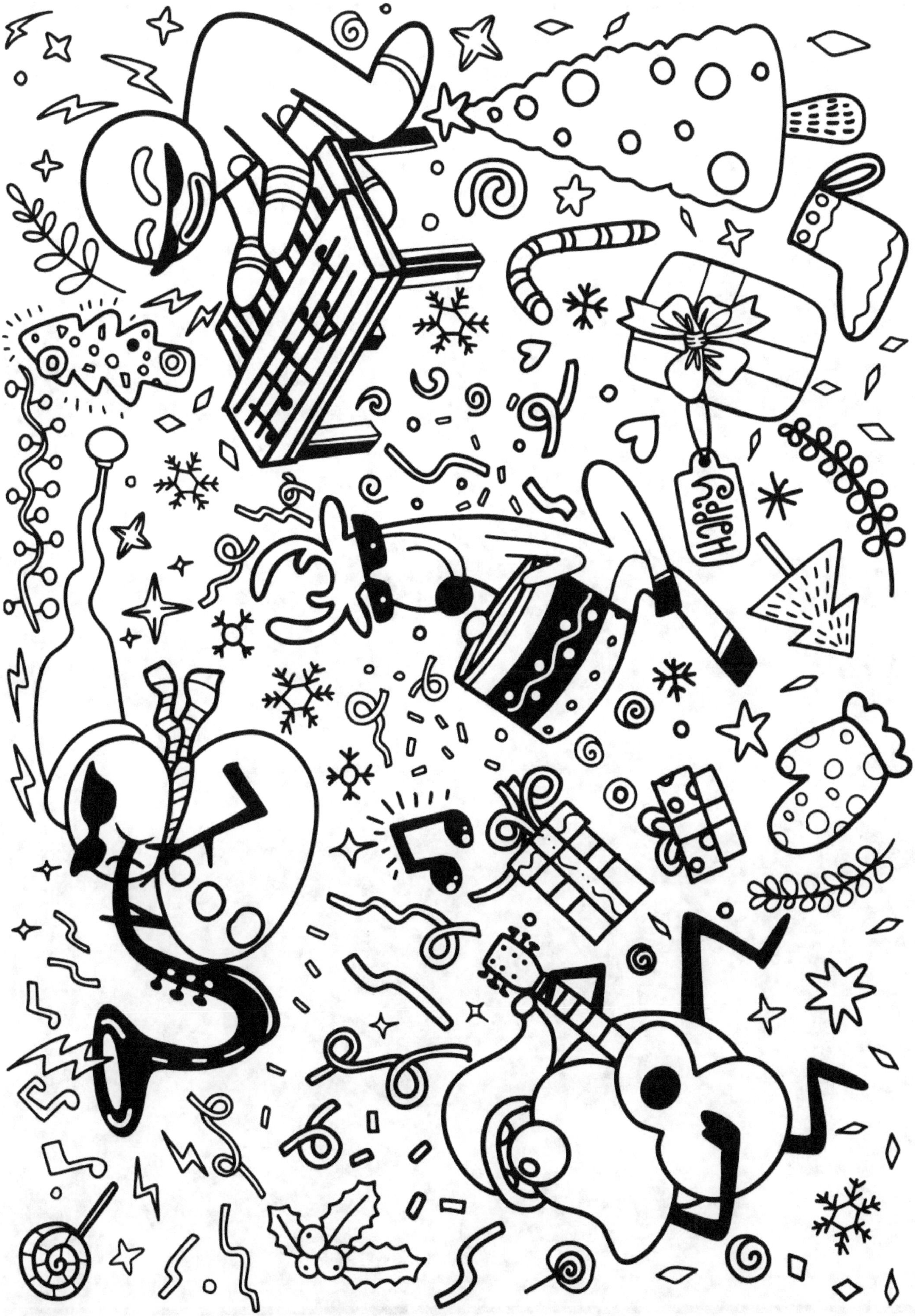
Happy

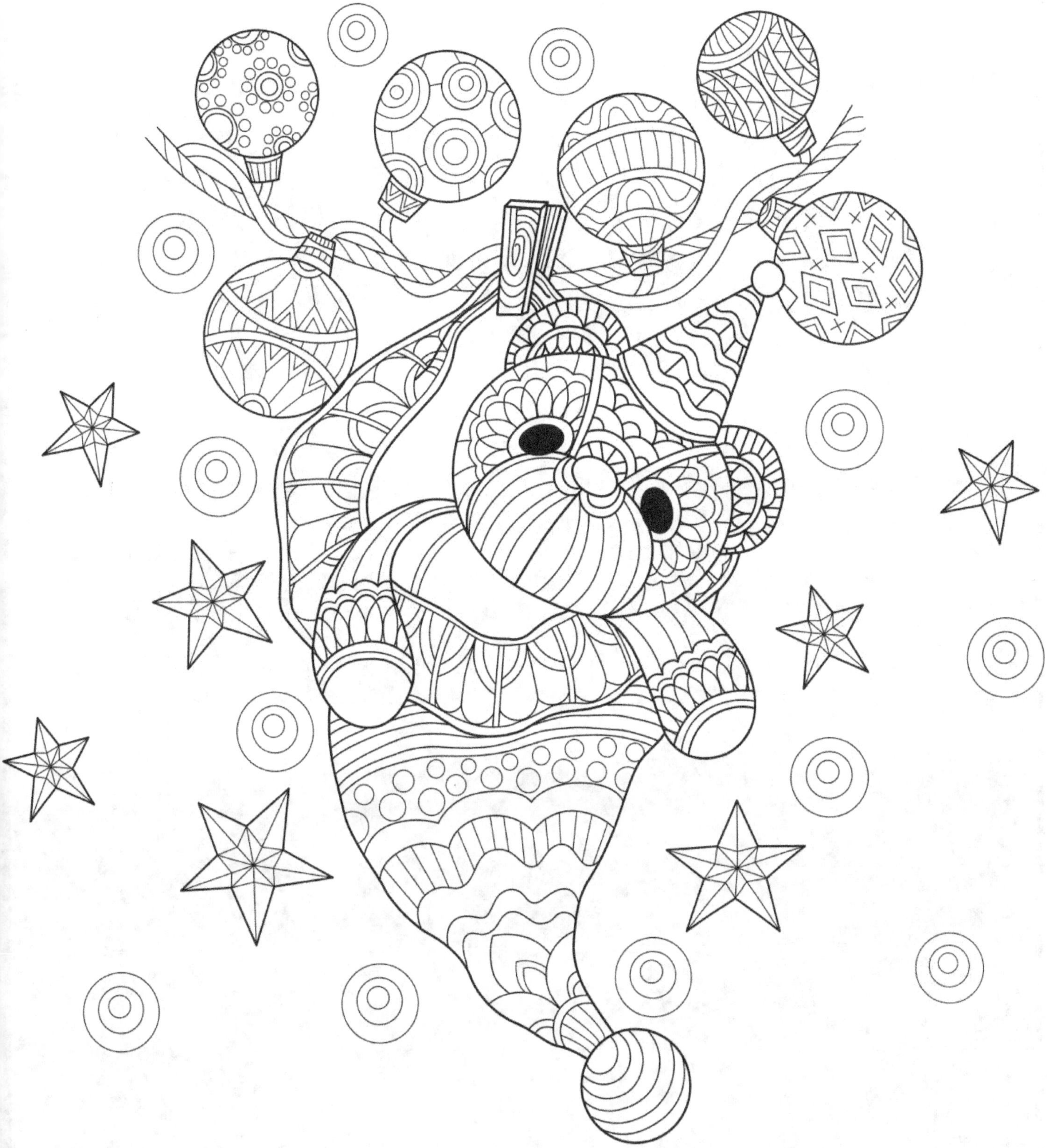

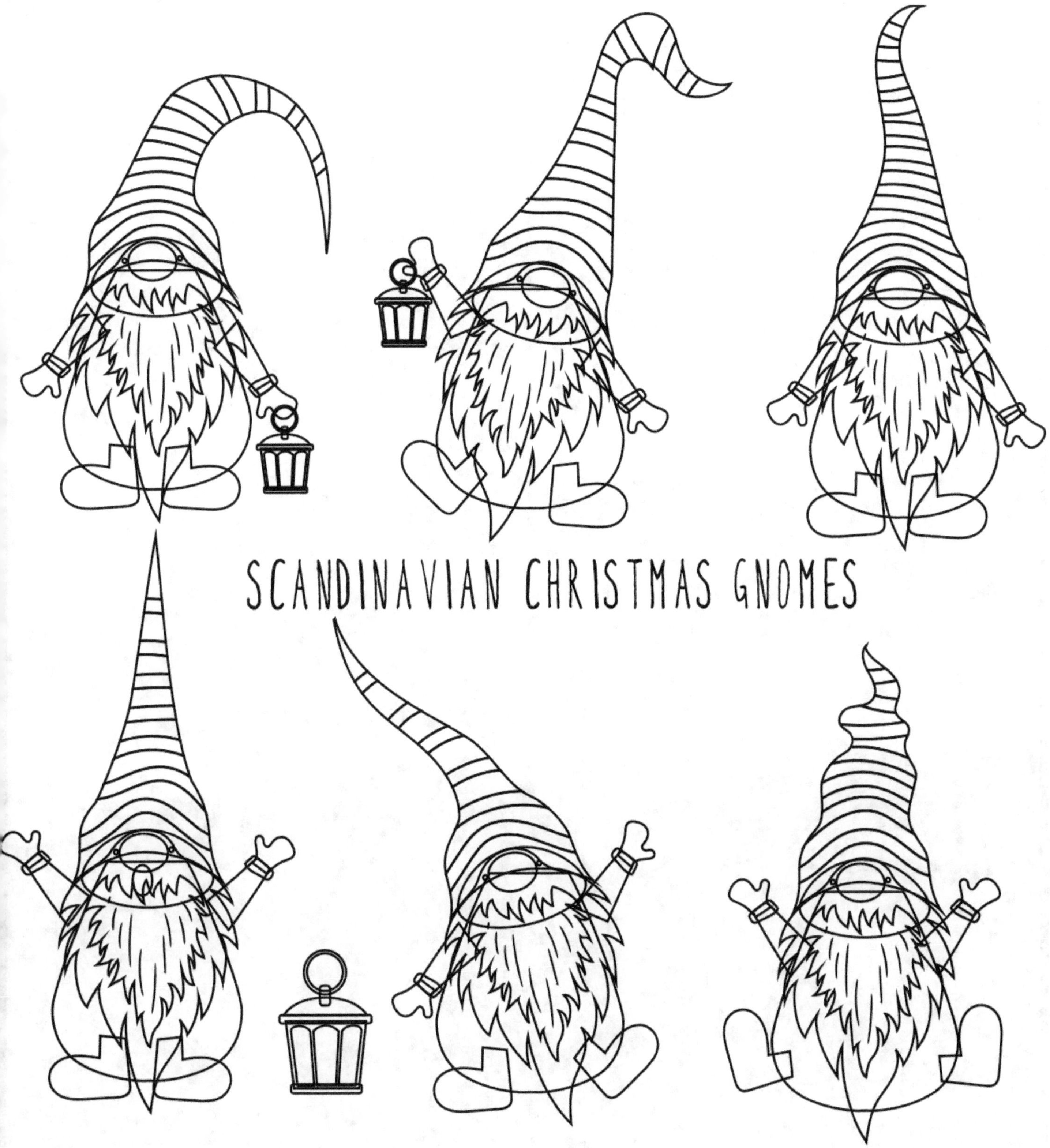
SCANDINAVIAN CHRISTMAS GNOMES

www.ingramcontent.com/pod-product-compliance
Lightning Source LLC
Chambersburg PA
CBHW081543220526
45467CB00010B/3311
* 9 7 8 1 7 0 5 4 7 2 3 7 8 *